CHANAKYA NEETI:

WITH THE COMPLETE SUTRAS

Chanakya was an ancient Indian teacher, philosopher, economist, jurist and royal advisor. He is traditionally identified as Kauṭilya or Vishnugupta, who authored the ancient Indian political treatise, the Arthashastra, a text dated to roughly between the 2nd century BCE and the 3rd century CE. As such, he is considered the pioneer of the field of political science and economics in India, and his work is thought of as an important precursor to classical economics. His works were lost near the end of the Gupta Empire and not rediscovered until the early twentieth century.

Contents

Chanakya Neeti teaches us about the Ideal Way of living the life and shows Chanakya's Deep Study of Indian Way of life.

It is said that Chanakya had been personally offended by King Nanda and that this powerful brahmana had vowed to keep his long sikha unknotted until he saw to the demise of the contemptuous ruler and his drunken princes. True to his oath, it was only after Chanakya Pandit engineered a swift death for the degraded and worthless rulers of the Nanda dynasty that this great brahmana was able to again tie up his tuft of hair. There are several versions relating the exact way that Chanakya had set about eliminating the Nandas, and it appears historians have found it difficult to separate fact from folk legend as regards to certain specific details.

With the dual obstacles of the Nandas and Alexander's troops out of the way, Chanakya Pandit used every political device and intrigue to unite the greater portion of the Indian sub-continent. Under the Prime ministership of Chanakya, King Chandragupta Maurya conquered all the lands up to Iran in the North west and down to the extremities of Karnataka or Mysore state in the South. It was by his wits alone that this skinny and ill-clad brahmana directed the formation of the greatest Indian empire ever before seen in history (ie. since the beginning of Kali-yuga). Thus the indigenous Vedic culture of the sacred land of Bharata was protected and the spiritual practices of the Hindus could go on unhampered.

Chanakya assisted the first Mauryan emperor Chandragupta in his rise to power. He is widely credited for having played an important role in the establishment of the Maurya Empire. Chanakya served as the chief advisor to both Emperors Chandragupta and his son Bindusara.

Although many great savants of the science of niti such as Brihaspati, Shukracharya, Bhartrihari and Vishnusharma have echoed many of these instructions in their own celebrated works*, it is perhaps the way that Chanakya applied his teachings of niti-sastra that has made him stand out as a significant historical figure. The great Pandit teaches us that lofty ideals can become a certain reality if we intelligently work towards achieving our goal in a determined, progressive and practical manner.

CHAPTER ONE

1. Humbly bowing down before the almighty Lord Sri Vishnu, the Lord of the three worlds, I recite maxims of the science of political ethics (niti) selected from the various shaastras.

2. That man who by the study of these maxims from the shaastras acquires a knowledge of the most celebrated principles of duty, and understands what ought and what ought not to be followed, and what is good and what is bad, is most excellent.

3. Therefore with an eye to the public good, I shall speak that which, when understood, will lead to an understanding of things in their proper perspective.

4. Even a pandit comes to grief by giving instruction to a foolish disciple, by maintaining a wicked wife, and by excessive familiarity with the miserable.

5. A wicked wife, a false friend, a saucy servant and living in a house with a serpent in it are nothing but death.

6. One should save his money against hard times, save his wife at the sacrifice of his riches, but invariably one should save his soul even at the sacrifice of his wife and riches.

7. Save your wealth against future calamity. Do not say, "What fear has a rich man of calamity?" When riches begin to forsake one even the accumulated

stock dwindles away.

8. Do not inhabit a country where you are not respected, cannot earn your livelihood, have no friends, or cannot acquire knowledge.

9. Do not stay for a single day where there are not these five persons: a wealthy man, a brahmin well versed in Vedic lore, a king, a river and a physician.

10. Wise men should never go into a country where there are no means of earning one's livelihood, where the people have no dread of anybody, have no sense of shame, no intelligence, or a charitable disposition.

11. Test a servant while in the discharge of his duty, a relative in difficulty, a friend in adversity, and a wife in misfortune.

12. He is a true friend who does not forsake us in time of need, misfortune, famine, or war, in a king's court, or at the crematorium (shmashaan).

13. He who gives up what is imperishable for that which perishable, loses that which is imperishable; and doubtlessly loses that which is perishable also.

14. A wise man should marry a virgin of a respectable family even if she is deformed. He should not marry one of a low-class family, through beauty. Marriage in a family of equal status is preferable.

15. Do not put your trust in rivers, men who carry weapons, beasts with claws or horns, women, and members of a royal family.

16. Even from poison extract nectar, wash and take back gold if it has fallen in filth, receive the highest knowledge (Krsna consciousness) from a low born person; so also a girl possessing virtuous qualities (stri-ratna) even if she be born in a disreputable family.

17. Women have hunger two-fold, shyness four-fold, daring six-fold, and lust eight-fold as compared to men.

CHAPTER TWO

1. Untruthfulness, rashness, guile, stupidity, avarice, uncleanliness and cruelty are women's seven natural flaws.

2. To have ability for eating when dishes are ready at hand, to be robust and virile in the company of one's religiously wedded wife, and to have a mind for making charity when one is prosperous are the fruits of no ordinary austerities.

3. He whose son is obedient to him, whose wife's conduct is in accordance with his wishes, and who is content with his riches, has his heaven here on earth.

4. They alone are sons who are devoted to their father. He is a father who supports his sons. He is a friend in whom we can confide, and she only is a wife in whose company the husband feels contented and peaceful.

5. Avoid him who talks sweetly before you but tries to ruin you behind your back, for he is like a pitcher of poison with milk on top.

6. Do not put your trust in a bad companion nor even trust an ordinary friend, for if he should get angry with you, he may bring all your secrets to light.

7. Do not reveal what you have thought upon doing, but by wise council keep it secret being determined to carry it into execution.

8. Foolishness is indeed painful, and verily so is youth, but more painful by far than either is being obliged in another person's house.

9. There does not exist a ruby in every mountain, nor a pearl in the head of every elephant; neither are the sadhus to be found everywhere, nor sandal trees in every forest.

10. (Note: Only Elephants in royal palaces are seen decorated with Pearls (Precious Stones) on their heads).

11. Wise men should always bring up their sons in various moral ways, for children who have knowledge of niti-shaastra and are well-behaved become a glory to their family.

12. Those parents who do not educate their sons are their enemies; for as is a crane among swans, so are ignorant so are ignorant sons in a public assembly.

13. Many a bad habit is developed through overindulgence, and many a good one by chastisement, therefore beat your son as well as your pupil; never indulge them. ("Spare the rod and spoil the child.")

14. Let not a single day pass without your learning a verse, half a verse, or a fourth of it, or even one letter of it; nor without attending to charity, study and other pious activity.

15. Separation from the wife, disgrace from one's

own people, an enemy saved in battle, service to a wicked king, poverty, and a mismanaged assembly: these six kinds of evils, if afflicting a person, burn him even without fire.

16. Trees on a river bank, a woman in another man's house, and kings without counsellors go without doubt to swift destruction.

17. A Brahmin's strength is in his learning, a king's strength is in his army, a vaishya's strength is in his wealth and a shudra's strength is in his attitude of service.

18. The prostitute has to forsake a man who has no money, the subject a king that cannot defend him, the birds in a tree that bears no fruit, and the guests in a house after they have finished their meals.

19. Brahmins quit their patrons after receiving alms from them, scholars leave their teachers after receiving education from them, and animals desert a forest that has been burnt down.

20. He who befriends a man whose conduct is vicious, whose vision impure, and who is notoriously crooked, is rapidly ruined.

21. Friendship between Equal's flourishes, service under a king is respectable, it is good to be business-minded in public dealings, and a handsome lady is safe in her own home.

CHAPTER THREE

1. In this world, whose family is there without blemish? Who is free from sickness and grief? Who is forever happy?

2. A man's descent may be discerned by - his conduct, his country by his pronunciation of language, his friendship by his warmth and glow, and his capacity to eat by his body.

3. Give your daughter in marriage to a good family, engage your son in learning, see that your enemy comes to grief, and engage your friends in dharma. (Krsna consciousness).

4. Of a rascal and a serpent, the serpent is the better of the two, for he strikes only at the time he is destined to kill, while the former at every step.

5. Therefore kings gather round themselves men of good families, for they never forsake them either at the beginning, the middle or the end.

6. At the time of the pralaya (universal destruction) the oceans are to exceed their limits and seek to change, but a saintly man never changes.

7. Do not keep company with a fool for as we can see he is a two-legged beast. Like an unseen thorn he pierces the heart with his sharp words.

8. Though men be endowed with beauty and youth and born in noble families, yet without education they are like the palasa flower which is void of

sweet fragrance.

9. The beauty of a cuckoo is in its notes, that of a woman in her unalloyed devotion to her husband, that of an ugly person in his scholarship, and that of an ascetic in his forgiveness.

10. Give up a member to save a family, a family to save a village, a village to save a country, and the country to save yourself.

11. There is no poverty for the industrious. Sin does not attach itself to the person practicing japa (chanting of the holy names of the Lord). Those who are absorbed in maunam (silent contemplation of the Lord) have no quarrel with others. They are fearless who remain always alert.

12. What is too heavy for the strong and what place is too distant for those who put forth effort? What country is foreign to a man of true learning? Who can be inimical to one who speaks pleasingly?

13. As a whole forest becomes fragrant by the existence of a single tree with sweet-smelling blossoms in it, so a family becomes famous by the birth of a virtuous son.

14. As a single withered tree, if set aflame, causes a whole forest to burn, so does a rascal son destroy a whole family.

15. As night looks delightful when the moon shines, so is a family gladdened by even one learned and

virtuous son.

16. What is the use of having many sons if they cause grief and vexation? It is better to have only one son from whom the whole family can derive support and peacefulness.

17. Fondle a son until he is five years of age, and use the stick for another ten years, but when he has attained his sixteenth year treat him as a friend.

18. He who runs away from a fearful calamity, a foreign invasion, a terrible famine, and the companionship of wicked men is safe.

19. He who has not acquired one of the following: religious merit (dharma), wealth (artha), satisfaction of desires (kama), or liberation (moksa) is repeatedly born to die.

20. Lakshmi, the Goddess of wealth, comes of Her own accord where fools are not respected, grain is well stored up, and the husband and wife do not quarrel.

CHAPTER FOUR

1. These five: the life-span, the type of work, wealth, learning and the time of one's death are determined while one is in the womb.

2. Offspring, friends and relatives flee from a devotee of the Lord: yet those who follow him bring merit to their families through their devotion.

3. Fish, tortoises, and birds bring up their young by means of sight, attention and touch; so do saintly men afford protection to their associates by the same means.

4. As long as your body is healthy and under control and death is distant, try to save your soul; when death is immanent what can you do?

5. Learning is like a cow of desire. It, like her, yields in all seasons. Like a mother, it feeds you on your journey. Therefore learning is a hidden treasure.

6. A single son endowed with good qualities is far better than a hundred devoid of them. For the moon, though one, dispels the darkness, which the stars, though numerous, cannot.

7. A still-born son as superior to a foolish son endowed with a long life. The first causes grief for but a moment while the latter like a blazing fire consumes his parents in grief for life.

8. Residing in a small village devoid of proper living facilities, serving a person born of a low family,

unwholesome food, a frowning wife, a foolish son, and a widowed daughter burn the body without fire.

9. What good is a cow that neither gives milk nor conceives? Similarly, what is the value of the birth of a son if he becomes neither learned nor a pure devotee of the Lord?

10. When one is consumed by the sorrows of life, three things give him relief: offspring, a wife, and the company of the Lord's devotees.

11. Kings speak for once, men of learning once, and the daughter is given in marriage once. All these things happen once and only once.

12. Religious austerities should be practiced alone, study by two, and singing by three. A journey should be undertaken by four, agriculture by five, and war by many together.

13. She is a true wife who is clean (suci), expert, chaste, pleasing to the husband, and truthful.

14. The house of a childless person is a void, all directions are void to one who has no relatives, the heart of a fool is also void, but to a poverty stricken man all is void.

15. Scriptural lessons not put into practice are poison; a meal is poison to him who suffers from indigestion; a social gathering is poison to a poverty stricken person; and a young wife is poison to an aged man.

16. That man who is without religion and mercy should be rejected. A guru without spiritual knowledge should be rejected. The wife with an offensive face should be given up, and so should relatives who are without affection.

17. Constant travel brings old age upon a man; a horse becomes old by being constantly tied up; lack of sexual contact with her husband brings old age upon a woman; and garments become old through being left in the sun.

18. Consider again and again the following: the right time, the right friends, the right place, the right means of income, the right ways of spending, and from whom you derive your power.

19. For the twice-born the fire (Agni) is a representative of God. The Supreme Lord resides in the heart of His devotees. Those of average intelligence (alpa-buddhi or kanista-adhikari) see God only in His Sri-murti, but those of broad vision see the Supreme Lord everywhere.

CHAPTER FIVE

1. Agni is the worshipable person for the twice-born; the brahmana for the other castes; the husband for the wife; and the guest who comes for food at the midday meal for all.

2. As gold is tested in four ways by rubbing, cutting, heating and beating -- so a man should be tested by these four things: his renunciation, his conduct, his qualities and his actions.

3. A thing may be dreaded as long as it has not overtaken you, but once it has come upon you, try to get rid of it without hesitation.

4. Though persons be born from the same womb and under the same stars, they do not become alike in disposition as the thousand fruits of the badari tree.

5. He whose hands are clean does not like to hold an office; he who desires nothing cares not for bodily decorations; he who is only partially educated cannot speak agreeably; and he who speaks out plainly cannot be a deceiver.

6. The learned are envied by the foolish; rich men by the poor; chaste women by adulteresses; and beautiful ladies by ugly ones.

7. Indolent application ruins study; money is lost when entrusted to others; a farmer who sows his seed sparsely is ruined; and an army is lost for want of a commander.

8.   Learning is retained through putting into practice; family prestige is maintained through good behaviour; a respectable person is recognised by his excellent qualities; and anger is seen in the eyes.

9.   Religion is preserved by wealth; knowledge by diligent practice; a king by conciliatory words; and a home by a dutiful housewife.

10.   Those who blaspheme Vedic wisdom, who ridicule the life style recommended in the shaastras, and who deride men of peaceful temperament, come to grief unnecessarily.

11.   Charity puts an end to poverty; righteous conduct to misery; discretion to ignorance; and scrutiny to fear.

12.   There is no disease (so destructive) as lust; no enemy like infatuation; no fire like wrath; and no happiness like spiritual knowledge.

13.   A man is born alone and dies alone; and he experiences the good and bad consequences of his karma alone; and he goes alone to hell or the Supreme abode.

14.   Heaven is but a straw to him who knows spiritual life (Krsna consciousness); so is life to a valiant man; a woman to him who has subdued his senses; and the universe to him who is without attachment for the world.

15.   Learning is a friend on the journey; a wife in the

house; medicine in sickness; and religious merit is the only friend after death.

16. Rain which falls upon the sea is useless; so is food for one who is satiated; in vain is a gift for one who is wealthy; and a burning lamp during the daytime is useless.

17. There is no water like rainwater; no strength like one's own; no light like that of the eyes; and no wealth more dear than food grain.

18. The poor wish for wealth; animals for the faculty of speech; men wish for heaven; and godly persons for liberation.

19. The earth is supported by the power of truth; it is the power of truth that makes the sun shine and the winds blow; indeed all things rest upon truth.

20. The Goddess of wealth is unsteady (chanchala), and so is the life breath. The duration of life is uncertain, and the place of habitation is uncertain; but in all this inconsistent world religious merit alone is immovable.

21. Among men the barber is cunning; among birds the crow; among beasts the jackal; and among women, the malin (flower girl).

22. These five are your fathers; he who gave you birth, girdled you with sacred thread, teaches you, provides you with food, and protects you from fearful situations.

23. These five should be considered as mothers; the king's wife, the preceptor's wife, the friend's wife, your wife's mother, and your own mother.

CHAPTER SIX

1. By means of hearing one understands dharma, malignity vanishes, knowledge is acquired, and liberation from material bondage is gained.

2. Among birds the crow is vile; among beasts the dog; the ascetic whose sins is abominable, but he who blasphemes others is the worst chandala.

3. Brass is polished by ashes; copper is cleaned by tamarind; a woman, by her menses; and a river by its flow.

4. The king, the brahmana, and the ascetic yogi who go abroad are respected; but the woman who wanders is utterly ruined.

5. He who has wealth has friends. He who is wealthy has relatives. The rich one alone is called a man, and the affluent alone are respected as pandits.

6. As is the desire of Providence, so functions one's intellect; one's activities are also controlled by Providence; and by the will of Providence one is surrounded by helpers.

7. Time perfects all living beings as well as kills them; it alone is awake when all others are asleep. Time is insurmountable.

8. Those born blind cannot see; similarly blind are those in the grip of lust. Proud men have no perception of evil; and those bent on acquiring riches see no sin in their actions.

9. The spirit soul goes through his own course of karma and he himself suffers the good and bad results thereby accrued. By his own actions he entangles himself in samsara, and by his own efforts he extricates himself.

10. The king is obliged to accept the sins of his subjects; the purohit (priest) suffers for those of the king; a husband suffers for those of his wife; and the guru suffers for those of his pupils.

11. A father who is a chronic debtor, an adulterous mother, a beautiful wife, and an unlearned son are enemies (in one's own home).

12. Conciliate a covetous man by means of a gift, an obstinate man with folded hands in salutation, a fool by humouring him, and a learned man by truthful words.

13. It is better to be without a kingdom than to rule over a petty one; better to be without a friend than to befriend a rascal; better to be without a disciple than to have a stupid one; and better to be without a wife than to have a bad one.

14. How can people be made happy in a petty kingdom? What peace can we expect from a rascal friend? What happiness can we have at home in the company of a bad wife? How can renown be gained by instructing an unworthy disciple?

15. Learn one thing from a lion; one from a crane; four from a cock; five from a crow; six from a dog; and three from an ass.

16. The one excellent thing that can be learned from a lion is that whatever a man intends doing should be done by him with a whole-hearted and strenuous effort.

17. The wise man should restrain his senses like the crane and accomplish his purpose with due knowledge of his place, time and ability.

18. To wake at the proper time; to take a bold stand and fight; to make a fair division (of property) among relations; and to earn one's own bread by personal exertion are the four excellent things to be learned from a cock.

19. Union in privacy (with one's wife); boldness; storing away useful items; watchfulness; and not easily trusting others; these five things are to be learned from a crow.

20. Contentment with little or nothing to eat although one may have a great appetite; to awaken instantly although one may be in a deep slumber; unflinching devotion to the master; and bravery; these six qualities should be learned from the dog.

21. Although an ass is tired, he continues to carry his burden; he is unmindful of cold and heat; and he is always contented; these three things should be learned from the ass.

22. He who shall practice these twenty virtues shall become invincible in all his undertakings.

CHAPTER SEVEN

1. A wise man should not reveal his loss of wealth, the vexation of his mind, the misconduct of his own wife, base words spoken by others, and disgrace that has befallen him.

2. He who gives up shyness in monetary dealings, in acquiring knowledge, in eating and in business, becomes happy.

3. The happiness and peace attained by those satisfied by the nectar of spiritual tranquillity is not attained by greedy persons restlessly moving here and there.

4. One should feel satisfied with the following three things; his own wife, food given by Providence and wealth acquired by honest effort; but one should never feel satisfied with the following three; study, chanting the holy names of the Lord (Japa) and charity.

5. Do not pass between two Brahmanas, between a brahmana and his sacrificial fire, between a wife and her husband, a master and his servant, and a plough and an ox.

6. Do not let your foot touch fire, the spiritual master or a brahmana; it must never touch a cow, a virgin, an old person or a child.

7. Keep one thousand cubits away from an elephant, a hundred from a horse, ten from a horned beast, but keep away from the wicked by leaving the

country.

8. An elephant is controlled by a goad (ankusha), a horse by a slap of the hand, a horned animal with the show of a stick, and a rascal with a sword.

9. Brahmanas find satisfaction in a good meal, peacocks in the peal of thunder, a sadhu in seeing the prosperity of others, and the wicked in the misery of others.

10. Conciliate a strong man by submission, a wicked man by opposition, and the one whose power is equal to yours by politeness or force.

11. The power of a king lies in his mighty arms; that of a brahmana in his spiritual knowledge; and that of a woman in her beauty youth and sweet words.

12. Do not be very upright in your dealings for you would see by going to the forest that straight trees are cut down while crooked ones are left standing.

13. Swans live wherever there is water, and leave the place where water dries up; let not a man act so -- and come and go as he pleases.

14. Accumulated wealth is saved by spending just as incoming fresh water is saved by letting out stagnant water.

15. He who has wealth has friends and relations; he alone survives and is respected as a man.

16. The following four characteristics of the denizens of heaven may be seen in the residents of this earth planet; charity, sweet words, worship of the Supreme Personality of Godhead, and satisfying the needs of brahmanas.

17. The following qualities of the denizens of hell may characterise men on earth; extreme wrath, harsh speech, enmity with one's relations, the company with the base, and service to men of low extraction.

18. By going to the den of a lion pearls from the head of an elephant may be obtained; but by visiting the hole of a jackal nothing but the tail of a calf or a bit of the hide of an ass may found.

19. The life of an uneducated man is as useless as the tail of a dog which neither covers its rear end, nor protects it from the bites of insects.

20. Purity of speech, of the mind, of the senses, and the of a compassionate heart are needed by one who desires to rise to the divine platform.

21. As you seek fragrance in a flower, oil in the sesamum seed, fire in wood, ghee (Butter) in milk, and jaggery (guda) in sugarcane; so seek the spirit that is in the body by means of discrimination.

CHAPTER EIGHT

1. Low class men desire wealth; middle class men both wealth and respect; but the noble, honour only; hence honour is the noble man's true wealth.

2. The lamp eats up the darkness and therefore it produces lamp black; in the same way according to the nature of our diet (sattva, rajas, or tamas) we produce offspring in similar quality.

3. O wise man! Give your wealth only to the worthy and never to others. The water of the sea received by the clouds is always sweet. The rain water enlivens all living beings of the earth both movable (insects, animals, humans, etc.) and immovable (plants, trees, etc.), and then returns to the ocean it value multiplied a million fold.

4. The wise who discern the essence of things have declared that the yavana (meat eater) is equal in baseness to a thousand candalas the lowest class), and hence a yavana is the basest of men; indeed there is no one more base.

5. After having rubbed oil on the body, after encountering the smoke from a funeral pyre, after sexual intercourse, and after being shaved, one remains a chandala until he bathes.

6. Water is the medicine for indigestion; it is invigorating when the food that is eaten is well digested; it is like nectar when drunk in the middle of a dinner; and it is like poison when

taken at the end of a meal.

7. 7. Knowledge is lost without putting it into practice; a man is lost due to ignorance; an army is lost without a commander; and a woman is lost without a husband.

8. A man who encounters the following three is unfortunate; the death of his wife in his old age, the entrusting of money into the hands of relatives, and depending upon others for food.

9. Chanting of the Vedas without making ritualistic sacrifices to the Supreme Lord through the medium of Agni, and sacrifices not followed

10. by bountiful gifts are futile. Perfection can be achieved only through devotion (to the Supreme Lord) for devotion is the basis of all success.

11. There is no austerity equal to a balanced mind, and there is no happiness equal to contentment; there is no disease like covetousness, and no virtue like mercy.

12. Anger is a personification of Yama (the demigod of death); thirst is like the hellish river Vaitarani; knowledge is like a kamadhenu (the cow of plenty); and contentment is like Nandanavana (the garden of Indra).

13. Moral excellence is an ornament for personal beauty; righteous conduct, for high birth; success for learning; and proper spending for wealth.

14. Beauty is spoiled by an immoral nature; noble birth by bad conduct; learning, without being perfected; and wealth by not being properly utilised.

15. Water seeping into the earth is pure; and a devoted wife is pure; the king who is the benefactor of his people is pure; and pure is the brahmana who is contented.

16. Discontented brahmanas, contented kings, shy prostitutes, and immodest housewives are ruined.

17. Of what avail is a high birth if a person is destitute of scholarship? A man who is of low extraction is honoured even by the demigods if he is learned.

18. learned man is honoured by the people. A learned man commands respect everywhere for his learning. Indeed, learning is honoured everywhere.

19. Those who are endowed with beauty and youth and who are born of noble families are worthless if they have no learning. They are just like

20. the kimshuka blossoms (flowers of the palasa tree) which, though beautiful, have no fragrance.

21. The earth is encumbered with the weight of the flesh-eaters, wine-bibblers, dolts (Dull and Stupid) and blockheads, who are beasts in the form of men.

22. There is no enemy like a yajna (sacrifice) which consumes the kingdom when not attended by feeding on a large scale; consumes the priest when the chanting is not done properly; and consumes the yajaman (the responsible person) when the gifts are not made.

CHAPTER NINE

1. My dear child, if you desire to be free from the cycle of birth and death, then abandon the objects of sense gratification as poison. Drink instead the nectar of forbearance, upright conduct, mercy, cleanliness and truth.

2. Those base men who speak of the secret faults of others destroy themselves like serpents who stray onto anthills.

3. Perhaps nobody has advised Lord Brahma, the creator, to impart perfume to gold; fruit to the sugarcane; flowers to the sandalwood tree; wealth to the learned; and long life to the king.

4. Nectar (amrita) is the best among medicines; eating good food is the best of all types of material happiness; the eye is the chief among all organs; and the head occupies the chief position among all parts of the body.

5. No messenger can travel about in the sky and no tidings come from there. The voice of its inhabitants as never heard, nor can any contact be established with them. Therefore the brahmana who predicts the eclipse of the sun and moon which occur in the sky must be considered as a vidwan (man of great learning).

6. The student, the servant, the traveller, the hungry person, the frightened man, the treasury guard, and the steward: these seven ought to be awakened if they fall asleep.

7. The serpent, the king, the tiger, the stinging wasp, the small child, the dog owned by other people, and the fool: these seven ought not to be awakened from sleep.

8. Of those who have studied the Vedas for material rewards, and those who accept foodstuffs offered by shudras, what potency have they? They are just like serpents without fangs.

9. He who neither rouses fear by his anger, nor confers a favour when he is pleased can neither control nor protect. What can he do?

10. The serpent may, without being poisonous, raise high its hood, but the show of terror is enough to frighten people -- whether he be venomous or not.

11. Wise men spend their mornings in discussing gambling, the afternoon discussing the activities of women, and the night hearing about the activities of theft. (The first item above refers to the gambling of King Yuddhisthira, the great devotee of Krishna. The second item refers to the glorious deeds of mother Sita, the consort of Lord Ramachandra. The third item hints at the adorable childhood pastimes of Sri Krishna who stole butter from the elderly cowherd ladies of Gokula. Hence Chanakya Pandits advises wise persons to spend the morning absorbed in Mahabharata, the afternoon studying Ramayana, and the evening devotedly hearing the Srimad-Bhagvatam.)

12. By preparing a garland for a Deity with one's

own hand; by grinding sandal paste for the Lord with one's own hand; and by writing sacred texts with one's own hand -- one becomes blessed with opulence equal to that of Indra.

13. Poverty is set off by fortitude; shabby garments by keeping them clean; bad food by warming it; and ugliness by good behaviour.

CHAPTER TEN

1. One destitute of wealth is not destitute, he is indeed rich (if he is learned); but the man devoid of learning is destitute in every way.

2. We should carefully scrutinise that place upon which we step (having it ascertained to be free from filth and living creatures like insects, etc.); we should drink water which has been filtered (through a clean cloth); we should speak only those words which have the sanction of the shaastras; and do that act which we have carefully considered.

3. He who desires sense gratification must give up all thoughts of acquiring knowledge; and he who seeks knowledge must not hope for sense gratification. How can he who seeks sense gratification acquire knowledge, and he who possesses knowledge enjoy mundane sense pleasure?

4. What is it that escapes the observation of poets? What is that act women are incapable of doing? What will drunken people not prate? What will not a crow eat?

5. Fate makes a beggar a king and a king a beggar. He makes a rich man poor and a poor man rich.

6. The beggar is a miser's enemy; the wise counsellor is the fool's enemy; her husband is an adulterous wife's enemy; and the moon is the enemy of the thief.

7. Those who are destitute of learning, penance, knowledge, good disposition, virtue and benevolence are brutes wandering the earth in the form of men. They are burdensome to the earth.

8. Those that are empty-minded cannot be benefited by instruction. Bamboo does not acquire the quality of sandalwood by being associated with the Malaya Mountain.

9. What good can the scriptures do to a man who has no sense of his own? Of what use is as mirror to a blind man?

10. Nothing can reform a bad man, just as the posterious cannot become a superior part of the body though washed one hundred times.

11. By offending a kinsman, life is lost; by offending others, wealth is lost; by offending the king, everything is lost; and by offending a brahmana one's whole family is ruined.

12. It is better to live under a tree in a jungle inhabited by tigers and elephants, to maintain oneself in such a place with ripe fruits and spring water, to lie down on grass and to wear the ragged barks of trees than to live amongst one's relations when reduced to poverty.

13. The brahmana is like tree; his prayers are the roots, his chanting of the Vedas are the branches, and his religious act are the leaves. Consequently effort should be made to preserve his roots for if

the roots are destroyed there can be no branches or leaves.

14. My mother is Kamala devi (Lakshmi), my father is Lord Janardana (Vishnu), my kinsmen are the Vishnu-bhaktas (Vaisnavas) and, my homeland is all the three worlds.

15. (Through the night) a great many kinds of birds perch(Sit and rest) on a tree but in the morning they fly in all the ten directions. Why should we lament (Expression of sorrow) for that? (Similarly, we should not grieve when we must inevitably part company from our dear ones).

16. He who possesses intelligence is strong; how can the man that is unintelligent be powerful? The elephant of the forest having lost his senses by intoxication was tricked into a lake by a small rabbit. (This verse refers to a famous story from the niti-sastra called pancatantra compiled by the Pandit Vishnusharma 2500 years ago).

17. Why should I be concerned for my maintenance while absorbed in praising the glories of Lord Vishwambhara (Vishnu), the supporter of all? Without the grace of Lord Hari, how could milk flow from a mother's breast for a child's nourishment? Repeatedly thinking only in this way, O Lord of the Yadus, O husband of Lakshmi, all my time is spent in serving your Lotus feet.

CHAPTER ELEVEN

1. Generosity, pleasing address, courage and propriety of conduct are not acquired, but are inbred qualities.

2. He who forsakes his own community and joins another perishes as the king who embraces an unrighteous path.

3. The elephant has a huge body but is controlled by the Ankusha (goad): yet, is the goad as large as the elephant? A lighted candle banishes darkness: is the candle as vast as the darkness. A mountain is broken even by a thunderbolt: is the thunderbolt therefore as big as the mountain? No, he whose power prevails is really mighty; what is there in bulk?

4. He who is engrossed in family life will never acquire knowledge; there can be no mercy in the eater of flesh; the greedy man will not be truthful; and purity will not be found in a woman and a hunter.

5. The wicked man will not attain sanctity even if he is instructed in different ways, and the nim tree will not become sweet even if it is sprinkled from the top to the roots with milk and ghee.

6. Mental dirt cannot be washed away even by one-hundred baths in the sacred waters, just as a wine pot cannot be purified even by evaporating all the wine by fire.

7. It is not strange if a man reviles (Degrades) a thing of which he has no knowledge, just as a wild hunter's wife throws away the pearl that is found in the head of an elephant, and picks up a gunj(a type of seed which poor tribals wear as ornaments).

8. He who for one year eats his meals silently (inwardly meditating upon the Lord's prasadam); attains to the heavenly planets for a thousand crore of years. (Note: one crore equals ten million)

9. The student (Brahmacari) should completely renounce the following eight things -- his lust, anger, greed, desire for sweets, sense of decorating the body, excessive curiosity, excessive sleep, and excessive endeavour for bodily maintenance.

10. He alone is a true brahmana (dvija or "twice-born") who is satisfied with one meal a day, who has the six samskaras (or acts of purification such as garbhadhana, etc.) performed for him, and who cohabits with his wife only once in a month on an auspicious day after her menses.

11. The brahmana who is engrossed in worldly affairs, brings up cows and is engaged in trade is really called a vaishya.

12. The brahmana who deals in lac-die, articles, oil, indigo, silken cloth, honey, clarified butter, liquor, and flesh is called a shudra.

13. The brahmana who thwarts the doings of others,

who is hypocritical, selfish, and a deceitful hater, and while speaking mildly cherishes cruelty in his heart, is called a cat.

14. The brahmana who destroys a pond, a well, a tank, a garden and a temple is called a mleccha.

15. The brahmana who steals the property of the Deities and the spiritual preceptor, who cohabits with another's wife, and who maintains himself by eating anything and everything is called a Chandala.

16. The meritorious should give away in charity all that they have in excess of their needs. By charity only Karna, Bali and King Vikramaditya survive even today. Just see the plight of the honeybees beating their legs in despair upon the earth. They are saying to themselves, "Alas! We neither enjoyed our stored-up honey nor gave it in charity, and now someone has taken it from us in an instant."

CHAPTER TWELVE

1. He is a blessed Grihasta (householder) in whose house there is a blissful atmosphere, whose sons are talented, whose wife speaks sweetly, whose wealth is enough to satisfy his desires, who finds pleasure in the company of his wife, whose servants are obedient, in whose house hospitality is shown, the auspicious Supreme Lord is worshiped daily, delicious food and drink is partaken, and who finds joy in the company of devotees.

2. One who devotedly gives a little to a Brahmana who is in distress is recompensed abundantly. Hence, O Prince, what is given to a good Brahmana is got back not in an equal quantity, but in an infinitely higher degree.

3. Those men who are happy in this world, who are generous towards their relatives, kind to strangers, indifferent to the wicked, loving to the good, shrewd in their dealings with the base, frank with the learned, courageous with enemies, humble with elders and stern with the wife.

4. O jackal, leave aside the body of that man at once, whose hands have never given in charity, whose ears have not heard the voice of learning, whose eyes have not beheld a pure devotee of the Lord, whose feet have never traversed to holy places, whose belly is filled with things obtained by crooked practices, and whose head is held high in vanity. Do not eat it, O jackal, otherwise you will become polluted.

5. "Shame upon those who have no devotion to the lotus feet of Sri Krishna, the son of mother Yasoda; who have no attachment for the describing the glories of Srimati Radharani; whose ears are not eager to listen to the stories of the Lord's lila." Such is the exclamation of the Mridanga sound of dhik-tam dhik-tam dhigatam at kirtana.

6. What fault of spring that the bamboo shoot has no leaves? What fault of the sun if the owl cannot see during the daytime? Is it the fault of the clouds if no raindrops fall into the mouth of the chatak bird? Who can erase what Lord Brahma has inscribed upon our foreheads at the time of birth?

7. A wicked man may develop saintly qualities in the company of a devotee, but a devotee does not become impious in the company of a wicked person. The earth is scented by a flower that falls upon it, but the flower does not contact the odour of the earth.

8. One indeed becomes blessed by having darshan of a devotee; for the devotee has the ability to purify immediately, whereas the sacred tirtha gives purity only after prolonged contact.

9. A stranger asked a brahmana, "Tell me, who is great in this city?" The brahmana replied, "The cluster of palmyra trees is great." Then the traveller asked, "Who is the most charitable person?" The brahmana answered, "The washerman who takes the clothes in the morning and gives them back in the evening is the most charitable." He then asked, "Who is the ablest man?" The brahmana

answered, "Everyone is expert in robbing others of their wives and wealth." The man then asked the brahmana, "How do you manage to live in such a city?" The brahmana replied, "As a worm survives while even in a filthy place so do I survive here!"

10. The house in which the lotus feet of brahmanas are not washed, in which Vedic mantras are not loudly recited, and in which the holy rites of Svaha (sacrificial offerings to the Supreme Lord) and Swadha (offerings to the ancestors) are not performed, is like a crematorium.

11. (It is said that a sadhu, when asked about his family, replied thusly): truth is my mother, and my father is spiritual knowledge; righteous conduct is my brother, and mercy is my friend, inner peace is my wife, and forgiveness is my son: these six are my kinsmen.

12. Our bodies are perishable, wealth is not at all permanent and death is always nearby. Therefore we must immediately engage in acts of merit.

13. Arjuna says to Krishna. "Brahmanas find joy in going to feasts, cows find joy in eating their tender grass, wives find joy in the company of their husbands, and know, O Krishna, that in the same way I rejoice in battle.

14. He who regards another's wife as his mother, the wealth that does not belong to him as a lump of mud, and the pleasure and pain of all other Living beings as his own -- truly sees things in the right perspective, and he is a true pandit.

15. O Raghava, the love of virtue, pleasing speech, and an ardent desire for performing acts of charity, guileless dealings with friends, humility in the guru's presence , deep tranquillity of mind, pure conduct, discernment of virtues, realised knowledge of the shaastras, beauty of form and devotion to God are all found in you." (The great sage Vasistha Muni, the spiritual preceptor of the dynasty of the sun, said this to Lord Ramachandra at the time of His proposed coronation).

16. The desire tree is wood; the golden Mount Meru is motionless; the wish-fulfilling gem cintamani is just a stone; the sun is scorching; the moon is prone to wane; the boundless ocean is saline; the demigod of lust lost his body (due to Shiva's wrath); Bali Maharaja, the son of Diti, was born into a clan of demons; and Kamadhenu (the cow of heaven) is a mere beast. O Lord of the Raghu dynasty! I cannot compare you to any one of these (taking their merits into account).

17. Realised learning (vidya) is our friend while travelling , the wife is a friend at home, medicine is the friend of a sick man, and meritorious deeds are the friends at death.

18. Courtesy should be learned from princes, the art of conversation from Pandits, lying should be learned from gamblers and deceitful ways should be learned from women.

19. The unthinking spender, the homeless urchin, the quarrel monger, the man who neglects his wife and is heedless in his actions -- all these will soon come to ruination.

20. The wise man should not be anxious about his food; he should be anxious to be engaged only in dharma (Krishna consciousness). The food of each man is created for him at his birth.

21. He who is not shy in the acquisition of wealth, grain and knowledge, and in taking his meals, will be happy

22. As centesimal droppings will fill a pot so also are knowledge, virtue and wealth gradually obtained.

23. The man who remains a fool even in advanced age is really a fool, just as the Indra-Varuna fruit does not become sweet no matter how ripe it might become.

CHAPTER THIRTEEN

1. A man may live but for a moment, but that moment should be spent in doing auspicious deeds. It is useless living even for a kalpa (4,320,000 *1000 years) and bringing only distress upon the two worlds (this world and the next).

2. We should not fret for what is past, nor should we be anxious about the future; men of discernment deal only with the present moment.

3. It certainly is nature of the demigods, men of good character, and parents to be easily pleased. Near and distant relatives are pleased when they are hospitably received with bathing, food, and drink; and pandits are pleased with an opportunity for giving spiritual discourse.

4. Even as the unborn Babe is in the womb of his mother, these five are fixed as his life destiny: his life span, his activities, his acquisition of wealth and knowledge, and his time of death.

5. O see what a wonder it is! The doings of the great are strange: they treat wealth as light as a straw, yet, when they obtain it, they bend under its weight.

6. He who is overly attached to his family member's experiences fear and sorrow, for the root of all grief is attachment. Thus one should discard attachment to be happy.

7. He who is prepared for the future and he who

deals cleverly with any situation that may arise are both happy; but the fatalistic man who wholly depends on luck is ruined.

8. 8. If the king is virtuous, then the subjects are also virtuous. If the king is sinful, then the subjects also become sinful. If he is mediocre, then the subjects are mediocre. The subjects follow the example of the king. In short, as is the king so are the subjects.

9. consider him who does not act religiously as dead though living, but he who dies acting religiously unquestionably lives long though he is dead.

10. He who has acquired neither virtue, wealth, satisfaction of desires nor salvation (Dharma, Artha, Kama, Moksa), lives an utterly useless life, like the "nipples" hanging from the neck of a goat.

11. The hearts of base men burn before the fire of other's fame, and they slander them being themselves unable to rise to such a high position.

12. Excessive attachment to sense pleasures leads to bondage, and detachment from sense pleasures leads to liberation; therefore it is the mind alone that is responsible for bondage or liberation.

13. He who sheds bodily identification by means of knowledge of the indwelling Supreme Self (Paramatma), will always be absorbed in meditative trance (samadhi) wherever his mind leads him.

14. Who realises all the happiness he desires? Everything is in the hands of God. Therefore one should learn contentment.

15. As a calf follows its mother among a thousand cows, so the (good or bad) deeds of a man follow him.

16. He whose actions are disorganised has no happiness either in the midst of men or in a jungle -- in the midst of men his heart burns by social contacts, and his helplessness burns him in the forest.

17. As the man who digs obtains underground water by use of a shovel, so the student attains the knowledge possessed by his preceptor through his service.

18. Men reap the fruits of their deeds, and intellects bear the mark of deeds performed in previous lives; even so the wise act after due circumspection.

19. Even the man who has taught the spiritual significance of just one letter ought to be worshiped. He who does not give reverence to such a guru is born as a dog a hundred times, and at last takes birth as a chandala (dog-eater).

20. At the end of the Yuga, Mount Meru may be shaken; at the end of the Kalpa, the waters of the seven oceans may be disturbed; but a sadhu will never swerve from the spiritual path.

21. There are three gems upon this earth; food, water, and pleasing words -- fools (mudhas) consider pieces of rocks as gems.

CHAPTER FOURTEEN

1. Poverty, disease, sorrow, imprisonment and other evils are the fruits borne by the tree of one's own sins.

2. ealth, a friend, a wife, and a kingdom may be regained; but this body when lost may never be acquired again.

3. The enemy can be overcome by the union of large numbers, just as grass through its collectiveness wards off erosion caused by heavy rainfall.

4. Oil on water, a secret communicated to a base man, a gift given to a worthy receiver, and scriptural instruction given to an intelligent man spread out by virtue of their nature.

5. If men should always retain the state of mind they experience when hearing religious instruction, when present at a crematorium ground, and when in sickness -- then who could not attain liberation.

6. If a man should feel before, as he feels after, repentance -- then who would not attain perfection?

7. We should not feel pride in our charity, austerity, valour, scriptural knowledge, modesty and morality for the world is full of the rarest gems.

8. He who lives in our mind is near though he may actually be far away; but he who is not in our

heart is far though he may really be nearby.

9. We should always speak what would please the man of whom we expect a favour, like the hunter who sings sweetly when he desires to shoot a deer.

10. It is ruinous to be familiar with the king, fire, the religious preceptor, and a woman. To be altogether indifferent of them is to be deprived of the opportunity to benefit ourselves; hence our association with them must be from a safe distance.

11. We should always deal cautiously with fire, water, women, foolish people, serpents, and members of a royal family; for they may, when the occasion presents itself, at once bring about our death.

12. He should be considered to be living who is virtuous and pious, but the life of a man who is destitute of religion and virtues is void of any blessing.

13. If you wish to gain control of the world by the performance of a single deed, then keep the following fifteen, which are prone to wander here and there, from getting the upper hand of you: the five sense objects (objects of sight, sound, smell, taste, and touch); the five sense organs (ears, eyes, nose, tongue and skin) and organs of activity (hands, legs, mouth, genitals and anus).

14. He is a Pandit (man of knowledge) who speaks what is suitable to the occasion, who renders

loving service according to his ability, and who knows the limits of his anger.

15. One single object (a woman) appears in three different ways: to the man who practices austerity it appears as a corpse, to the sensual it appears as a woman, and to the dogs as a lump of flesh.

16. A wise man should not divulge the formula of a medicine which he has well prepared; an act of charity which he has performed; domestic conflicts; private affairs with his wife; poorly prepared food he may have been offered; or slang he may have heard.

17. The cuckoos remain silent for a long time (for several seasons) until they are able to sing sweetly (in the spring) so as to give joy to all.

18. We should secure and keep the following: the blessings of meritorious deeds, wealth, grain, the words of the spiritual master, and rare medicines. Otherwise life becomes impossible.

19. Eschew (Avoid) wicked company and associate with saintly persons. Acquire virtue day and night, and always meditate on that which is eternal forgetting that which is temporary.

CHAPTER FIFTEEN

1. For one whose heart melts with compassion for all creatures; what is the necessity of knowledge, liberation, matted hair on the head, and smearing the body with ashes.

2. There is no treasure on earth the gift of which will cancel the debt a disciple owes his guru for having taught him even a single letter (that leads to Krishna consciousness).

3. There are two ways to get rid of thorns and wicked persons; using footwear in the first case and in the second shaming them so that they cannot raise their faces again thus keeping them at a distance.

4. He who wears unclean garments, has dirty teeth, as a glutton, speaks unkindly and sleeps after sunrise -- although he may be the greatest personality -- will lose the favour of Lakshmi.

5. He who loses his money is forsaken by his friends, his wife, his servants and his relations; yet when he regains his riches those who have forsaken him come back to him. Hence wealth is certainly the best of relations.

6. Sinfully acquired wealth may remain for ten years; in the eleventh year it disappears with even the original stock.

7. A bad action committed by a great man is not censured (as there is none that can reproach

him), and a good action performed by a low-class man comes to be condemned (because none respects him). Just see: the drinking of nectar is excellent, but it became the cause of Rahu's demise; and the drinking of poison is harmful, but when Lord Shiva (who is exalted) drank it, it became an ornament to his neck (nila-kanta).

8. A true meal is that which consists of the remnants left after a Brahmana's meal. Love which is shown to others is true love not that which is cherished for one's own self. To abstain from sin is true wisdom. That is an act of charity which is performed without ostentation.

9. For want of discernment the most precious jewels lie in the dust at the feet of men while bits of glass are worn on their heads. But we should not imagine that the gems have sunk in value, and the bits of glass have risen in importance. When a person of critical judgement shall appear, each will be given its right position.

10. Sastric knowledge is unlimited, and the arts to be learned are many; the time we have is short, and our opportunities to learn are beset with obstacles. Therefore select for learning that which is most important, just as the swan drinks only the milk in water.

11. He is a Chandala who eats his dinner without entertaining the stranger who has come to his house quite accidentally, having travelled from a long distance and is wearied.

12. One may know the four Vedas and the Dharma-

sastras, yet if he has no realisation of his own spiritual self, he can be said to be like the ladle which stirs all kinds of foods but knows not the taste of any.

13. Those blessed souls are certainly elevated who, while crossing the ocean of life, take shelter of a genuine Brahmana, who is likened unto a boat. They are unlike passengers aboard an ordinary ship which runs the risk of sinking.

14. The moon, who is the abode of nectar and the presiding deity of all medicines, although immortal like Amrta and resplendent in form, loses the brilliance of his rays when he repairs to the abode of the sun (day time). Therefore will not an ordinary man be made to feel inferior by going to live at the house of another.

15. This humble bee, who always resides among the soft petals of the lotus and drinks abundantly its sweet nectar, is now feasting on the flower of the ordinary kutaja. Being in a strange country where the lotuses do not exist, he is considering the pollen of the kutaja to be nice.

16. (Lord Visnu asked His spouse Lakshmi why She did not care to live in the house of a brahmana, when She replied) " O Lord, A rishi named Agastya drank up My father (the ocean) in anger; Brighu Muni kicked You; brahmanas pride themselves on their learning having sought the favour of My competitor Sarasvati; and lastly they pluck each day the

17. lotus which is My abode, and therewith worship

Lord Shiva. Therefore, O Lord, I fear to dwell with a brahmana and that properly.

18. There are many ways of binding by which one can be dominated and controlled in this world, but the bond of affection is the strongest. For example, take the case of the humble bee which, although expert at piercing hardened wood, becomes caught in the embrace of its beloved flowers (as the petals close at dusk).

19. Although sandalwood be cut, it does not forsake its natural quality of fragrance; so also the elephant does not give up sportiveness though he should grow old. The sugarcane does not cease to be sweet though squeezed in a mill; so the man of noble extraction does not lose his lofty qualities, no matter how pinched he is by poverty.

CHAPTER SIXTEEN

1. The heart of a woman is not united; it is divided. While she is talking with one man, she looks lustfully at another and thinks fondly of a third in her heart.

2. The fool (mudha) who fancies that a charming young lady loves him, becomes her slave and he dances like a shakuntal bird tied to a string.

3. Who is there who, having become rich, has not become proud? Which licentious (Free) man has put an end to his calamities (A grievous disaster)? Which man in this world has not been overcome by a woman? Who is always loved by the king? Who is there who has not been overcome by the ravages of time? Which beggar has attained glory? Who has become happy by contracting the vices of the wicked?

4. A man attains greatness by his merits, not simply by occupying an exalted seat. Can we call a crow an eagle (Garuda) simply because he sits on the top of a tall building.

5. The man who is praised by others as great is regarded as worthy though he may be really void of all merit. But the man who sings his own praises lowers himself in the estimation of others though he should be Indra (the possessor of all excellences).

6. If good qualities should characterise a man of discrimination, the brilliance of his qualities will

be recognised just as a gem which is essentially bright really shines when fixed in an ornament of gold.

7.   Even one who by his qualities appears to be all knowing suffers without patronage; the gem, though precious, requires a gold setting.

8.   I do not deserve that wealth which is to be attained by enduring much suffering, or by transgressing the rules of virtue, or by flattering an enemy.

9.   Those who were not satiated with the enjoyment of wealth, food and women have all passed away; there are others now passing away who have likewise remained unsatiated; and in the future still others will pass away feeling themselves unsatiated.

10. All charities and sacrifices (performed for fruitive gain) bring only temporary results, but gifts made to deserving persons (those who are Krishna consciousness) and protection offered to all creatures shall never perish.

11. A blade of grass is light, cotton is lighter, the beggar is infinitely lighter still. Why then does not the wind carry him away? Because it fears that he may ask alms of him.

12. It is better to die than to preserve this life by incurring disgrace. The loss of life causes but a moment's grief, but disgrace brings grief every day of one's life.

13. All the creatures are pleased by loving words;
    and therefore we should address words that are
    pleasing to all, for there is no lack of sweet words.

14. There are two nectarean fruits hanging from the
    tree of this world: one is the hearing of sweet
    words (such as Krishna-Katha) and the other, the
    society of saintly men.

15. The good habits of charity, learning and austerity
    practised during many past lives continue to be
    cultivated in this birth by virtue of the link (yoga)
    of this present life to the previous ones.

16. One whose knowledge is confined to books and
    whose wealth is in the possession of others can
    use neither his knowledge nor wealth when the
    need for them arises.

CHAPTER SEVENTEEN

1. The scholar who has acquired knowledge by studying innumerable books without the blessings of a bonafide spiritual master does not shine in an assembly of truly learned men just as an illegitimate child is not honoured in society.

2. We should repay the favours of others by acts of kindness; so also should we return evil for evil in which there is no sin, for it is necessary to pay a wicked man in his own coin.

3. That thing which is distant, that thing which appears impossible, and that which is far beyond our reach, can be easily attained through Tapasya (religious austerity), for nothing can surpass austerity.

4. What vice could be worse than covetousness? What is more sinful than slander? For one who is truthful, what need is there for austerity? For one who has a clean heart, what is the need for pilgrimage? If one has a good disposition, what other virtue is needed? If a man has fame, what is the value of other ornamentation? What need is there for wealth for the man of practical knowledge? And if a man is dishonoured, what could there be worse in death?

5. Though the sea, which is the reservoir of all jewels, is the father of the conch shell, and the Goddess of fortune Lakshmi is conch's sister, still the conch must go from door to door for alms (in the hands of a beggar). It is true, therefore, that

one gains nothing without having given in the past.

6. When a man has no strength left in him he becomes a sadhu, one without wealth acts like a Brahmachari, a sick man behaves like a devotee of the Lord, and when a woman grows old she becomes devoted to her husband.

7. There is poison in the fang of the serpent, in the mouth of the fly and in the sting of a scorpion; but the wicked man is saturated with it.

8. The woman who fasts and observes religious vows without the permission of her husband shortens his life, and goes to hell.

9. A woman does not become holy by offering by charity, by observing hundreds of fasts, or by sipping sacred water, as by sipping the water used to wash her husband's feet.

10. The hand is not so well adorned by ornaments as by charitable offerings; one does not become clean by smearing sandalwood paste upon the body as by taking a bath; one does not become so much satisfied by dinner as by having respect shown to him; and salvation is not attained by self-adornment as by cultivation of spiritual knowledge.

11. The eating of Tundi fruit deprives a man of his sense, while the vacha root administered revives his reasoning immediately. A woman at once robs a man of his vigour while milk at once restores it.

12. He who nurtures benevolence for all creatures within his heart overcomes all difficulties and will be the recipient of all types of riches at every step.

13. What is there to be enjoyed in the world of Lord Indra for one whose wife is loving and virtuous, who possesses wealth, who has a well-behaved son endowed with good qualities, and who has a grandchildren born of his children?

14. Men have eating, sleeping, fearing and mating in common with the lower animals. That in which men excel the beasts is discretionary knowledge; hence, indiscreet men who are without knowledge should be regarded as beasts.

15. If the bees which seek the liquid oozing from the head of a lust-intoxicated elephant are driven away by the flapping of his ears, then the elephant has lost only the ornament of his head. The bees are quite happy in the lotus filled lake.

16. A king, a prostitute, Lord Yamaraja, Fire, A Thief, A Young boy, and A Beggar cannot understand the suffering of others. The eighth of this category is the tax collector.

17. O lady, why are you gazing downward? Has something of yours fallen on the ground? (She replies) O fool, can you not understand the pearl of my youth has slipped away?

18. O ketki flower! Serpents live in your midst, you bear no edible fruits, your leaves are covered with

thorns, you are crooked in growth, you thrive in mud, and you are not easily accessible. Still for your exceptional fragrance you are as dear as a kinsmen to others. Hence, a single excellence overcomes a multitude of blemishes.